Mai ka Po Mai ka ʻOiaʻiʻo

Makakapu Ioane

© 2019 by Hinamalaelena Ioane

Pulled from the chant *He Kānaenae no Laka,* this excerpt means that from the dark ambiguousness comes truth. This motto is an encouragement to brave the unknown mysteries of the world.

O ke au o Makaliʻi ka po
During the time Makaliʻi has risen
O ka walewale hoʻokumu hōnua ia
Established slime that motivates lifes growth
O ke kumu o ka lipo, i lipo ai
The source of darkness, that invigorated darkness
O ke kumu o ka po i po ai
The source of night that produces night
O ka lipolipo, o ka lipolipo
The intense darkness, the intense darkness
O ka lipo o ka lā, o ka lipo o ka po
The darkness of the sun, the darkness of the night
Po wale hoʻi
There was only night
Hānau ka pō
The night gave birth
- Kumulipo

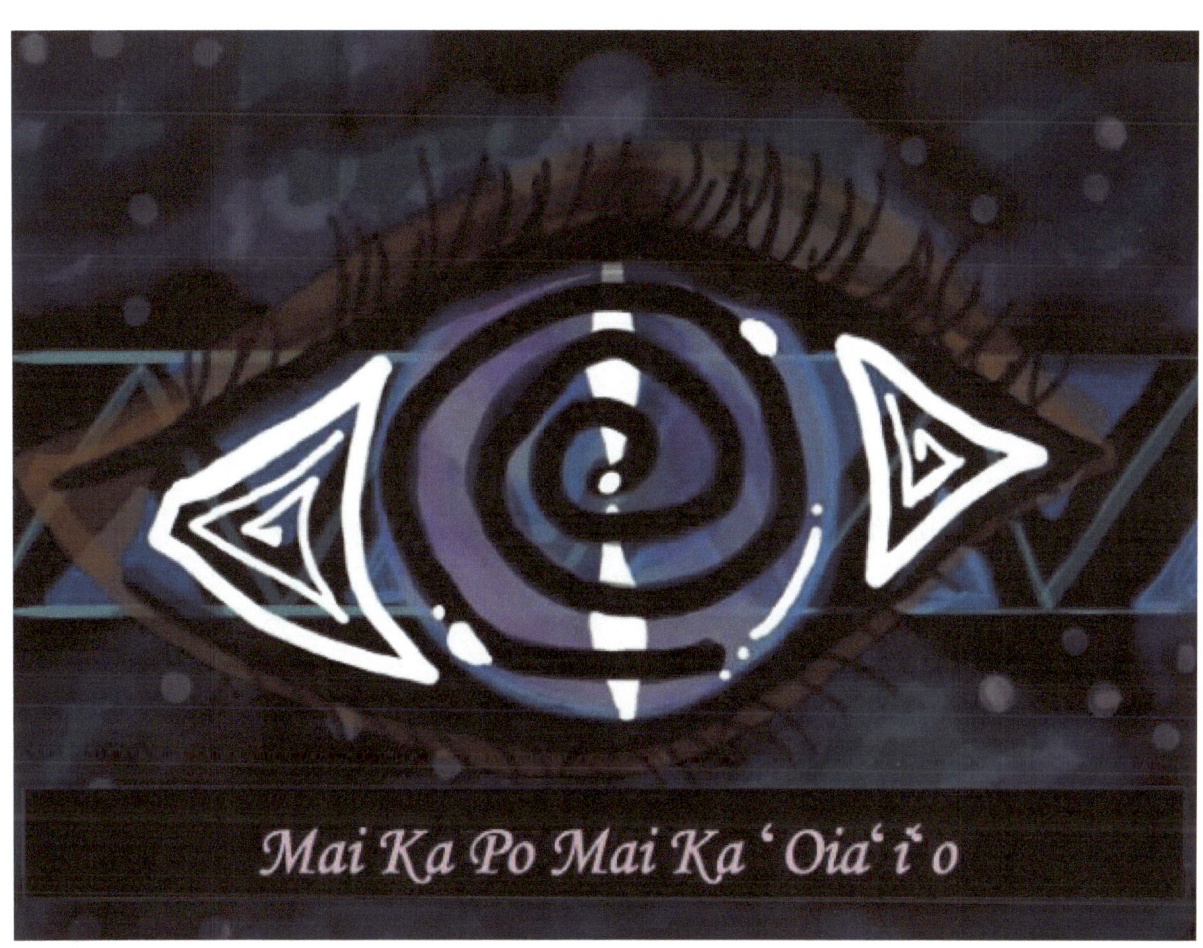

Chapter 1

Reaching Kapolaʻana

Within the ʻumeke
of vast ambiguousness
like the forest floor
on a moonless night
or the deepest depths of the ocean
to the naked human eye
there is kapo
the unseen
the continued subconscious
of ʻike kupuna
passed down to generations
of pua via the
night running through their veins
an ancient condensation
bleached of luminosity
to dam the precipitation
of ʻike kupuna
for the younger generations
- *Kapo the drive to hoʻomau*

ʻO Haumea, ʻO Mama ʻĀina

Environmental lineage
an umbilical cord
to the earth's evolutional
immortal heritage
Haumea birth giver
to the cycles of life
where science incorporates
spiritual and metaphysical superordinates
stars and plate tectonics
ordinate to the mandate of
Mama ʻāina

the mother of limitless fire
the spark and ember of creation
whose gravitational desire
elevates Hina and Kanehoalani higher
to an earthly and celestial dance

Hoʻokīkī Kānāwai

The birds that sing
in-tuned with the dancing trees
reflected in the afternoon breeze
here she hears the drumming beat
within her earthly fire,
desire beats, weather chums
the hearth of creation
stoked by Haʻihaʻilauahea
Lohiʻau invites her to dance

they fly within her
earthly realm
she, ablaze in birthing
new land to be filled
with potential abundances
of lush dancing trees
swaying to the melody
that the birds sing
reflected in the afternoon breeze

Laka Kumu Hula

I step into my church
I sing and dance
I praise the universe
Within my trance

the altar so beautiful
bountiful as the forest
Laka kumu hula
observant on her dias

a throne in my church
a palace beyond these walls
full of lively citizens
living the law of improvement
she is growth

my temple my home
a palace of its own
my sweat and dedication
a hoʻokupu to you

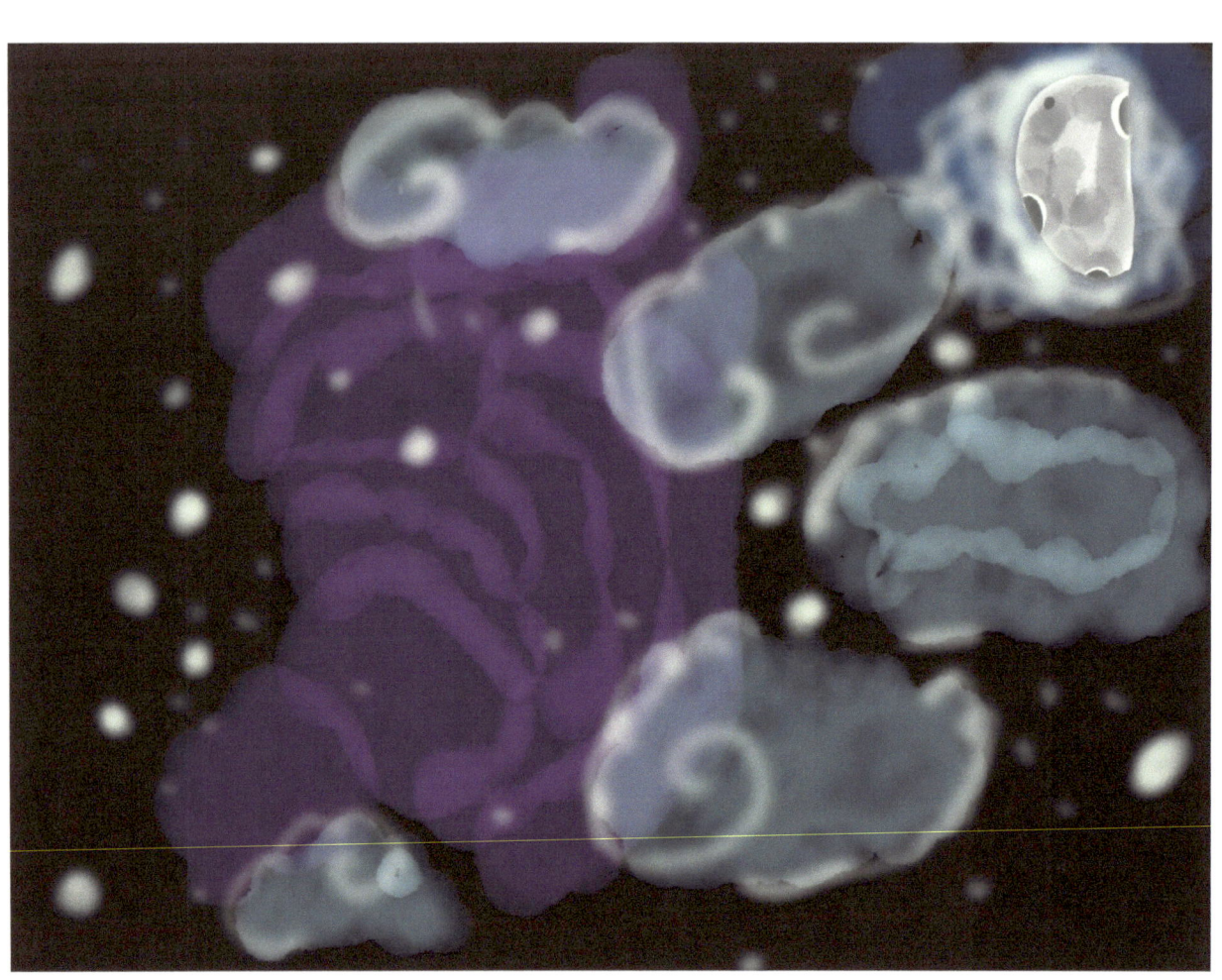

Kapo

Could you caress darkness
as if you were the stars
as if you were the light

essential darkness
like that of wombs
that of veins
running with nights
living silk

the void you enter
when you close your eyes
when you fall asleep at night

Kapo
the origin of ʻāina,
birthing darkness
the female's fire
to alight

The Wind

Is it cold?
Unlike sunlight
surrounding like water
cold like water
bitter and chilling
a stinging caress

a midnight feel
full of stars
on a sharp night
wading through its current

does it remind you
of the mountain peaks
vastly reaching for
a god or being
of the ocean
like the dark of caves
nurturing to life
of the shade in forests
relaxing such enticing
fingers to join peace

Papahulilani

Heavenly,
in tinges of
sunrise to sunset
time a repetitious
constant depicting
change by wind
pulling, pushing,
performing an immortal dance
of modeled creation
in a blunt cape of
the oceans hues
reflecting its mirrored
reflection in the realm
of gentleness whose
thoughts spiral repetitiously
to the beckoning beautiful
blinding darkness
back to the heavenly sunrise

Chapter 2

A Kū I Ke KaʻAi

Time reflecting strands
continuous moʻokuʻauhau of
past present and future generations

sacred rituals of hanauna
practiced and improved
from energy and time
from ʻōhiʻa lehua and ʻieʻie

Kihanuilulumoku
sacred chief of opening the rituals
for his posterity to uptake
in connecting lineage
to the environmental strands
reflected in time

Ka'ū 'Āina Kipi.

Once upon a time
in land of tradition
and gods reflected in nature
there lived a kaiaulu
located in the district of Ka'ū

the arid ruggedness of the land
was reflected within the people
and the people were the living voices
between dark and light

Ko'ihala, Kohaikalani, Hala'ea
chiefs of their time
ruling with greed
so their people
sunk, stoned, and smashed
their reign out of the earthly realm
Pipi holo ka'ao

He ʻInoa No Manono

Dressed as a man
with binded breast
and a mahiʻole
a warrior woman
descending as night
mai ka po mai
ka ʻoia ʻiʻo

responsibility a tattoo
masked on her face
ingrained in her naʻau
as she teaches
a battalion of fierce women
Pahoa lei o mano
cutting through
the fabric of time
to a Hawaiʻi
where aloha has to be re-learned

a spear in her hand
ahuʻula upon her shoulders
remnants of a deceased
husband, Kekuaokalani
as she charged into battle
taking her final breath
she chanted
Ko aloha la ʻea
Ko aloha la ʻea
Mālama ko aloha
Mālama ko aloha!
- *Keep the love for each other and this land*

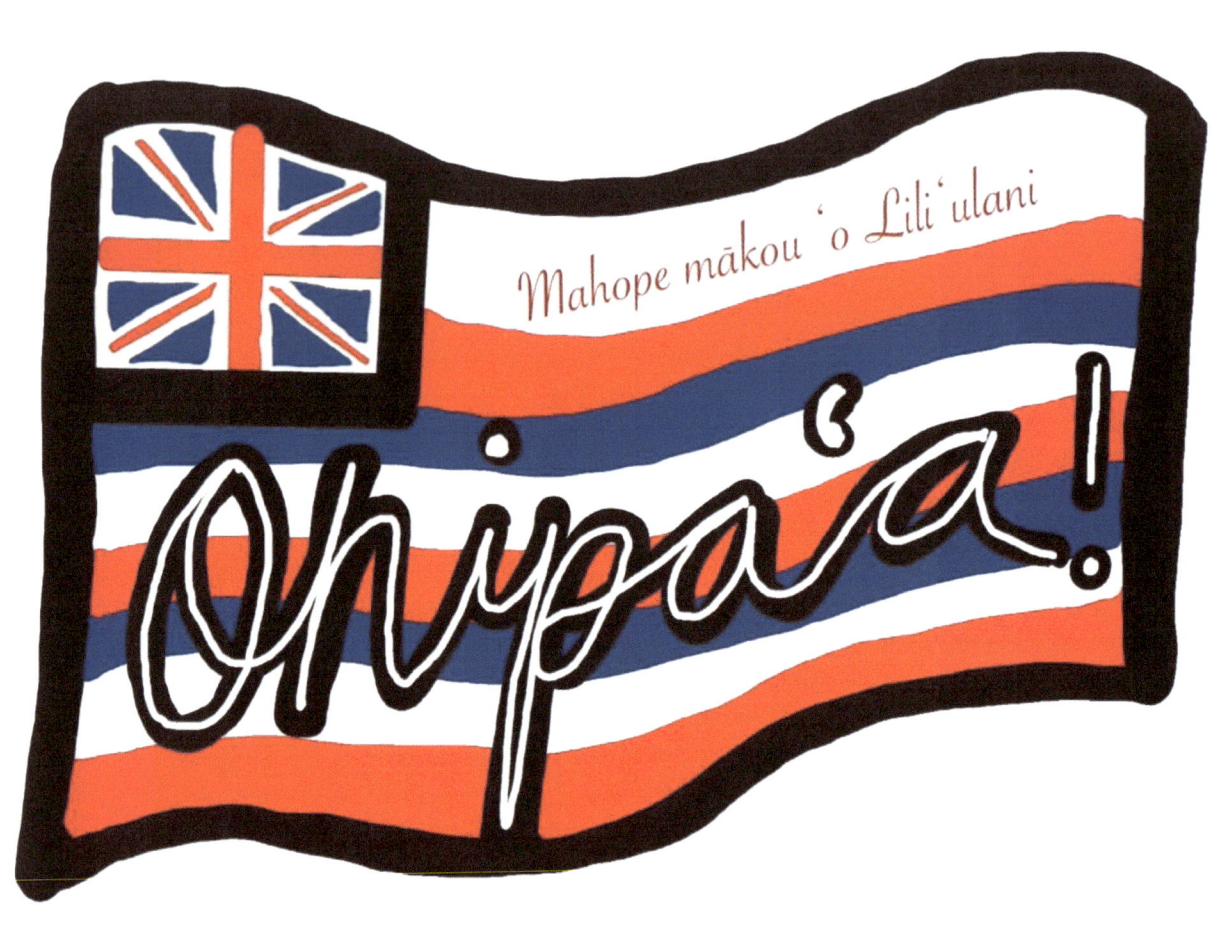

Kamakaʻeha

She knows pain
like lightning through
a broken heart
or fire on an open wound

wounding its way to her naʻau
as her people silently rage and cry
her name a prayer
sovereignty locked in a cell
with coral bars
and walls made of glass
this colonized imprisonment
a Kingdom forced to kneel

as we kneel in prayer
your strength our strength
Liliʻuokalani
our last reigning monarch

Chapter 3

Kuleana

In a vast forest
with mountains that roll
capped with lush greens
there is a pond

in a vast pond
with dark knowing waters
like the rain clouds obscuring the moon
there is a reflection

in a knowing reflection
there is an earth tinged girl
with nights hued hair
and generations of ancestors
looking back

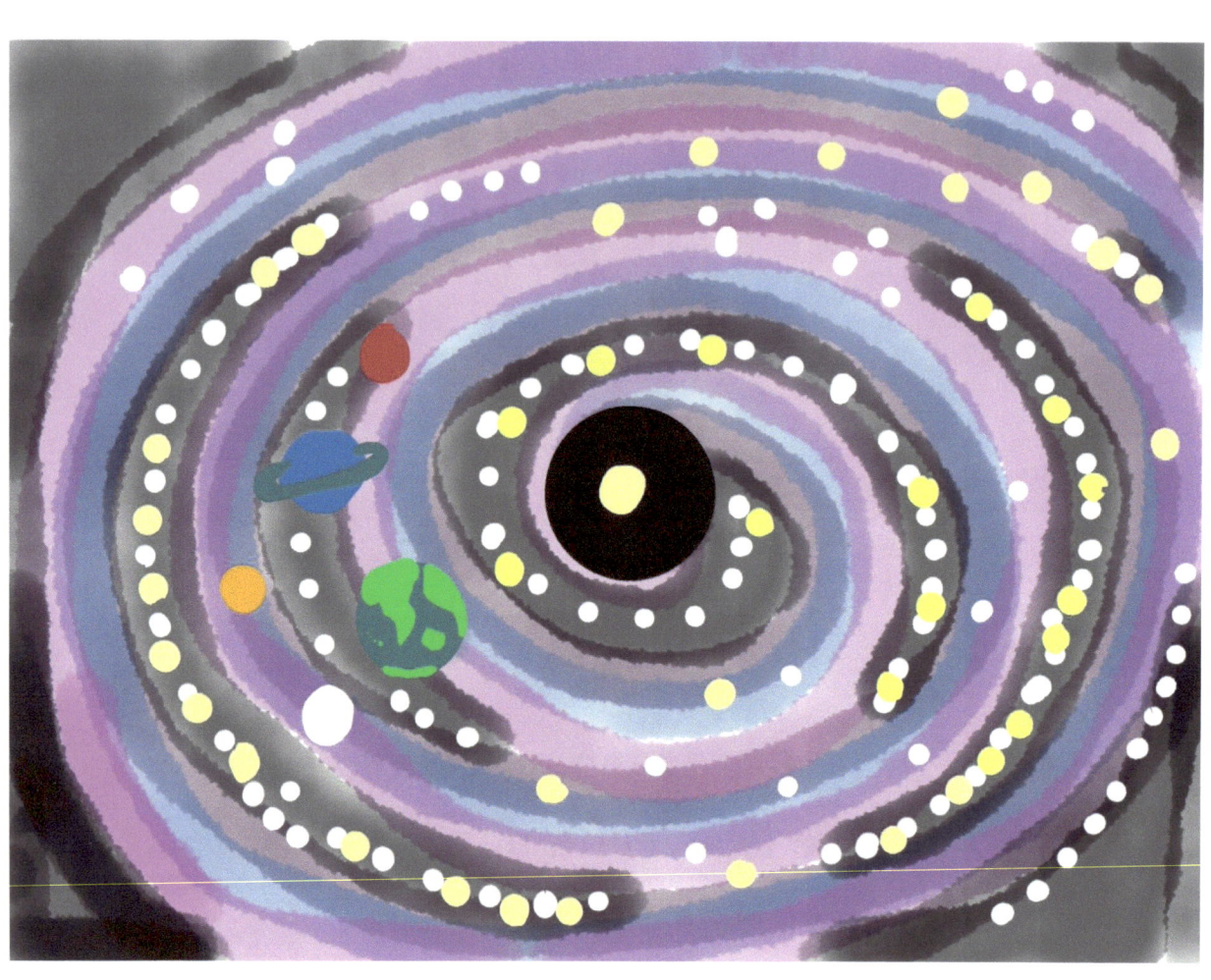

Realization

Recognize your place
within the megladonic
solar system
milking away at a universe
cycling through a spiral
called life
Death. Decaying time
rejuvenation through prayer
of vibrant greens, browns, whites,
pinks, blues, oranges, yellows, reds
like an image in the peak
of spring
wet rain pouring from
an invisible shield
broken and trapped
by those who do not
recognize themselves in this
place called earth

Somewhere Far Far Away

Pedals painted by sunrise
blending into the nights tide
bringing a home away from home

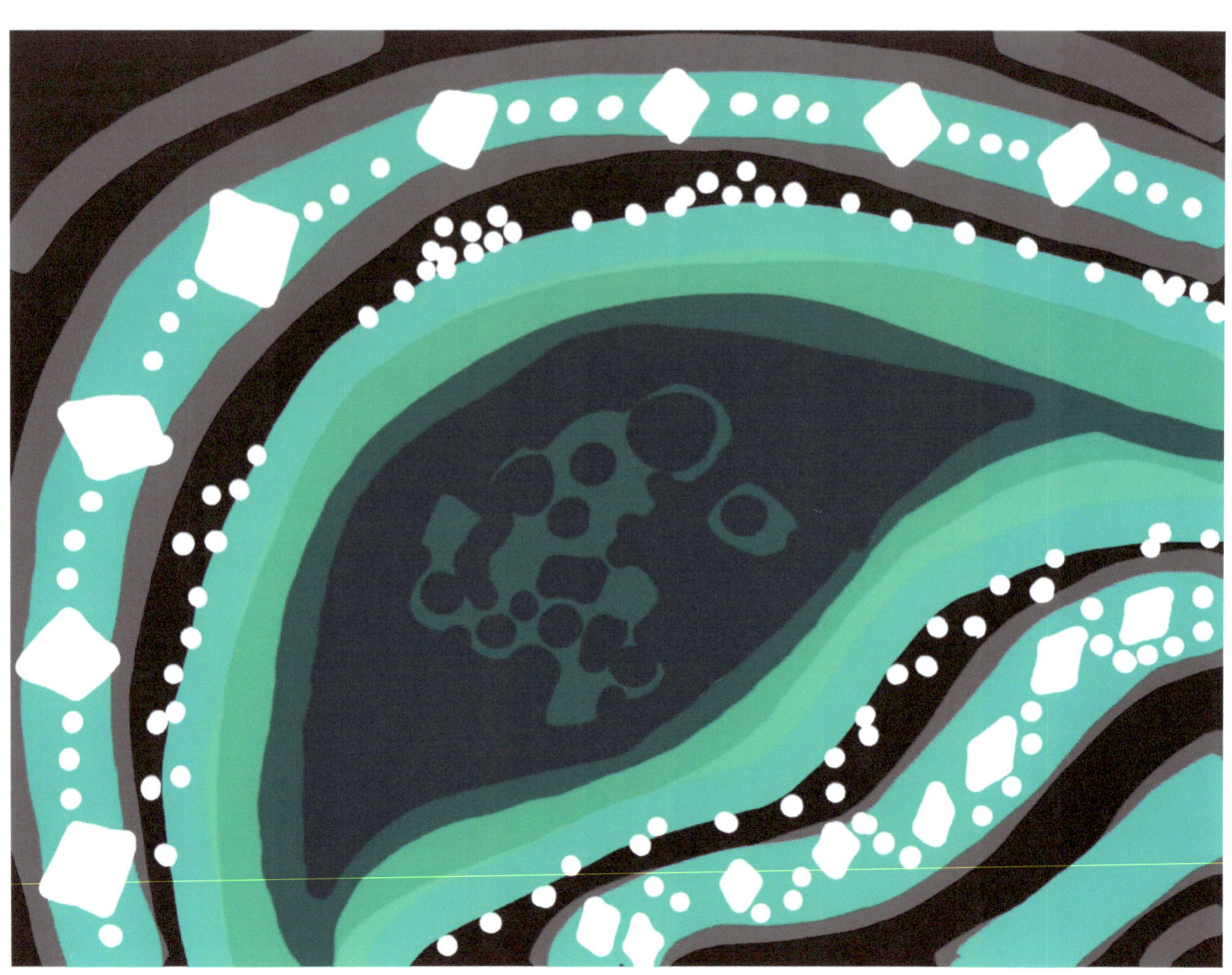

'Ōma'o Rivers

Emerald crystals
liquid gems
iced particles
recharging my skin
fresh scent
lively taste
rushing sounds
an energy burst!!

Beautiful Hawai'i

Her voice speaks to me
beautiful Hawai'i

her birds sing to me
about beautiful Hawai'i

her shores withdraw my soul from within me
to beautiful Hawai'i

her winds carry to me
reminding me of old beautiful Hawai'i

her fire blazes spreading heat of remanences
memories of beautiful Hawai'i

her fish swim in my dreams
flooding me with beautiful Hawai'i

her essence flows inside me
knowledge of beautiful Hawai'i

her rage burns through my mirrors
windows of beautiful Hawai'i

she says never forget me
never forget Beautiful Hawai'i

Kuleana Pt.2

Some people are too blind to fight
for anything that's right
right in front of their eyes

Restless Nights

I am rouge to
the thought of simplicity
but tranquility comes from listening
which I try that of no doubt
but with no words
all I could do is shout
from the top of my crown
to the dirt on my feet
content is far, even for me

Seasonal

Growing through
phases of abundance
and the lack thereof
like the full moon
and flowers in fall

Mountainous Waves

It takes elegance
to appear calm in raging waters

www.ingramcontent.com/pod-product-compliance
Lightning Source LLC
Chambersburg PA
CBHW042019150426
43197CB00002B/78